Barry Baddock & Susie Vrobel

Translation Skills

German – English
Lösungen

Ein abwechslungsreiches
Trainingsprogramm

Max Hueber Verlag

R 3. 2. | Die letzten Ziffern
2002 2001 2000 1999 | bezeichnen Zahl und Jahr des Druckes.
Alle Drucke dieser Auflage können, da unverändert,
nebeneinander benutzt werden.
1. Auflage

Umschlaggestaltung: Gerhard Rudauskas, München
Druck und Bindung: Ludwig Auer, Donauwörth
Printed in Germany
ISBN 3-19-012440-X

Introduction

First, a reminder. As we said at the start of *Translation Skills*, you should use this Answer Key only after attempting a particular exercise. You may make some mistakes, but you will steadily develop your translation abilities if you first try an exercise, and check the answers only afterwards.

Here are some guidelines on how to produce a competent and polished translation. After finishing a translation, read through it again and ask yourself...

1. 'Does my translation mean exactly the same as the original? Does it make sense in its own right? Is it logical?' If the answer to any of these questions is 'no, not really', then it can't be right and you should work through the translation again.
2. 'Does my translation contain gaps or missing words?' Obviously, these will be of no use to the reader! If you don't know the English word for die Bibliothek, it's far better to use a wordy expression like 'the building where books are kept' than to leave the word untranslated altogether!
3. 'Does my translation offer the reader alternative words?' An example: 'The memory of the affair (business, matter) made him laugh (smile)'. While this is not as bad as leaving words untranslated, it's frustrating for the reader and advertises your own uncertainty as a translator. Throughout the translation, commit yourself to one version only.
4. 'Is my translation readable as natural, normal English?' This will be difficult for you to judge if English is not your native language. But you could check through your translation to see if its sentence patterns and word order are slavish copies of the German structures. If they are, work through it again to see where you might improve on this phrasing or that point of style.
5. 'Is my translation well presented?' Don't abandon the rules of good writing in your effort to produce a good translation. Punctuate and capitalise it correctly throughout, produce it with the same paragraph arrangement, sub-headings and notation as the original and number the pages.

The grammar points treated in *Translation Skills* are 'danger areas' in which German translators of English often make mistakes. So, when you re-read your translation, pay special attention to these grammar points. You could work through it, first checking the articles, then the noun phrases and so on, until finally you have checked the structures of the completed sentences, as discussed in the final unit. This will involve a fair amount of work for you, but it is a sure way to achieve the goal of developing your translation skills.

Good luck!

Barry Baddock
Susie Vrobel

Unit 1: Articles

Lead-in

1-5 (all): no article!

Follow-up

1. He likes to play the guitar.
2. Do you play the violin too?
3. Would you repeat your accusations in the presence of witnesses?
4. A second television set is out of the question.
5. Even Martha, who was just 18 years old, was an atheist.
6. Mrs Russell was a convinced pacifist.
7. It's too threatening a situation to make further contingents available.
8. He was too intelligent a pupil to take part in demonstrations of that kind.
9. Patients infected with Ebola have a high temperature.
10. Suddenly life seemed worth living again.
11. Unemployment is a problem for the whole of Europe.
12. It's a danger to health.
13. From next month on, people in Munich have to pay more for beer.
14. Could we meet at Wilhelmshöhe Station at 5.00p.m.?
15. School cannot compensate for all the failings of the family.
16. At first sight, the precautionary measures seem groundless to me.
17. We'll discuss the rest after supper.

Consolidation

Dear Ms Fuchs,

As I've already told you on the phone, there is a possibility of supplementing Ms Baldwin's guest lecture in autumn this year with a second lecture. Ms Baldwin is a Canadian and works at the University of Montreal as a gene technician and immunologist. The additional lecture, on the subject of "Diabetes Susceptibility Genes", can be held on the following day, provided you agree with this. Too late a date would not allow Ms Baldwin to continue her lecture series in Germany without a break. Therefore, November is out of the question, as far as an alternative date is concerned.

Please arrange for Ms Baldwin to be picked up at Frankfurt Airport on Tuesday of next week. She is expected in the early afternoon (AA 231, 13.06h).

It's a pity that we won't now be seeing each other at the Frankfurt Symposium, as originally planned. It is likely to be some time before our curriculum is adopted – however, we mustn't lose patience.

My sincere thanks for your efforts, and I am sorry this change of plan has come at such short notice.

With best wishes,

Holger Preetz
Research Assistant

Take your pick

1. Access to the dockyards is no longer possible. (Or: … not possible any longer.)
2. As an astronaut, he may weigh no more than 78 kilos. (Or: … may not weigh more than …)
3. We intend to invite no more than 30 people. (Or: … don't intend to invite more than …)
4. Rapid economic growth is no longer the sole criterion of social progress. (Or: … not the sole criterion of social progress any longer.)

What else?

1. Fruit + vegetables
   On sale inside the shop
2. Wet paint
3. Attention
   Please keep dogs on a lead
4. High voltage
   Danger to life
5. Keep off the building site
   Parents will be held responsible for their children.

Unit 2: Noun phrases

Lead-in

1. (a)(iv) (b)(vi) (c)(iii) (d)(i) (e)(vii) (f)(v) (g)(ii)
2. A: (i) (iii) (v) B: (vi) (vii) C: (ii) (iv)

Follow-up

1.
Meinungsumfrage: opinion poll
Wohnungsnot: housing shortage
Geldfrage: question of money
Grenzfall: borderline case
Faustregel: rule of thumb
Ozonloch: ozone hole
Todesstrafe: death penalty
Menschenrechte: human rights
Lebenszeichen: sign of life
Schwerpunkt: centre of gravity
Eingangstest: entrance test

2.
a. a young man fearlessly facing the hardships of life
b. a young man who is now fearlessly facing the hardships of life
c. the figure which was invented by Charles Dickens as the main character of his book “A Christmas Carol”
d. the American-Russian Shuttle Flight, which would have been inconceivable years ago
e. an end to the episode which is not to be expected
f. an old but still completely useable typewriter

Consolidation

1. German subsidiary of
2. British group of companies
3. the disposal of asbestos
4. knowledge of English and German
5. secretarial and administrative responsibilities
6. telephone enquiries and conversations
7. small translation tasks
8. ability in shorthand and word-processing
9. construction or engineering matters
10. and salary expectations

Take your pick

1.
a. He declared his love for her.
b. She declared/explained that she had nothing to do with the matter.
c. She explained to him how a PC works.
d. In 1957, Ghana declared its/her independence.
e. He couldn't account for the accident.

2.
a. Becker will possibly/probably win the tournament without playing, as Muster had to go to hospital.
b. The train eventually reached Nürnberg half-an-hour late.
c. Possible malformations cannot be ruled out.
d. I've probably made a mess of the first exam.
e. Probably the workmen will come somewhat later.
f. Possibly my philosophy professor will get struck by lightning.

What else?

2.
Speed limit 15km/hr
within the hospital grounds

3.
Pedestrians: watch out for trams

4.
Exit
Keep clear at all times

5.
Loading & unloading
and
cyclists permitted
18.30 – 10.00

6.
Parking
in the spaces indicated only with a valid permit

Unit 3: Adjectives & adverbs

Lead-in

1. valuable	2. subtle	3. actually	4. directly	5. directly
6. directly	7. Similarly	8. direct	9. international	10. centrally

Follow-up

1. Yes, it's extendable … a. ideal for a large family;
   b. ideally constructed for a large family.
2. At first sight, Curacao reminds you/one of Holland most (of all).
3. It's best (of all) to visit the capital on (a) Saturday morning.
   Or: The capital is best visited on (a) Saturday morning
4. The reaction was just as vehement as it was surprising.
5. The new bridge had been vehemently demanded for years.
6. The red spot on Jupiter is approximately as big as our planet.
7. His illness disappeared just as quickly as it appeared.
8. Unfortunately, they didn't know that the mushrooms he had gathered were (exactly) as poisonous as last year's.
9. Nothing new was presented at the conference.
10. Despite the purely humanitarian aim of helping and doing a lot of good for people, the aid project resulted in a catastrophe.
11. Should anything unexpected happen, please let me know immediately.
12. The inhabitants of Cadiz Province are (the) most severely affected by the long drought.
13. The fat man was very well liked as a teacher.
14. Only the initiated were able to recite the holy tablets of the Easter Islands.
15. And again philosophers are arguing about the sublime.
16. We anticipate the improbable in order to prevent the unthinkable.
17. Without doubt, our striker was the faster.
18. I prefer to/would rather spend the afternoon in the planetarium than in the stadium.
19. After losing everything, she will be sure never to set foot in the casino again.
20. People will ask why nothing seems/seemed to have been done in the '90s.
21. The striped one makes you look slimmer.
22. For many investors, the period of their investment is just as important as the interest earned.
23. The stronger the economic relationships (are), the wider also (is) the possibility of better political cooperation.

Consolidation

1. Trinidad

1. lively	2. absolutely	3. beautiful	4. rapidly	5. wild
6. historical	7. best (or: best of all)	8. good	9. most important	

2. Jamaica

Of all (the) Caribbean Islands, Jamaica offers the visitor the most (or: has most to offer the visitor). It is well-developed, spacious and scenically varied (or: has great scenic variety). To be sure, anyone looking for a big-city atmosphere with all its cultural and social opportunities will be disappointed, as neither the capital Kingston nor any other city in Jamaica can offer this. On the other hand (or: Instead), the island obliges (or: will oblige) with well-tended, attractive tropical beaches and a wide range of sports on offer, extending from every imaginable kind of water sport to riding and to golf. Jamaica possesses some of the most beautiful golf courses in the Caribbean. The recreational facilities on offer are largely limited to the big hotels and holiday establishments.

Take your pick

a.
1. Actually, it was a case of (an) optical illusion.
2. For the current terms of admittance, you should consult the brochure.
3. There were actually no survivors to be found. (Or: Actually, no survivors could be found.)
4. Unfortunately, the prices shown in the catalogue are no longer current (or: valid).
5. In the current fax directory, you will find all new subscribers up to (and including) November of last year.

b.
1. The environmental project was received with lively interest by a wide public.
2. Boxers frequently exhibit a broad nose.
3. Broadly speaking, the increasing adaptability of different viruses (or: different viruses' increasing ability to adapt) represents a threat to humanity.
4. We need some wide sticking plaster for the sides/side sections.

What else?

a.	1. room	2. town centre	3. quiet, secluded	4. parking
b.	1. room	2. kitchen	3. bathroom	4. fitted kitchen
	5. to let	6. inclusive	7. deposit	

c. 1. furnished 2. room flat 3. to let 4. deposit

d. 1. rooms 2. kitchen 3. bathroom 4. attic (or: attic room/flat) 5. deposit

Unit 4: Time phrases

Lead-in

1. b.

2. **The first newborn giraffe for 32 years**
Great delight in Frankfurt Zoo. For the first time since 1964, there has been a new birth in the giraffe enclosure there. The small bull-giraffe was born on 2 January. While the mother was bred in Copenhagen Zoo, father Archibald was caught long ago in Kenya.

Follow-up

a.
1. "Me? No, I haven't used the toaster again since Sunday." (Note: since + point-in-time + present perfect)
2. At the moment he's playing tennis, but he might be able to help us later. (Note: At the moment + present continuous; time phrases at beginning and end)
3. Since 1990, he has been occupied with his book. (Note: since + point-in-time + present perfect)
4. In the last few years/In recent years, (the) cooperation between the two countries has been increasing. (Note: time phrase at beginning or end; present perfect (continuous))
5. We were in Canada for six weeks in 1985. (Note: simple past; for + period of time)
6. "A Christmas Carol" first appeared on 19 December 1843 and sold 6000 copies by Christmas. (Note: simple past; by + point-in-time; time phrase at beginning or end)
7. A flood of new enterprises are trying their luck in this market right now. (Note: time phrase at beginning or end; right now + present continuous)
8. He has been a branch manager for two years.(Note: for + period of time; present perfect)
9. In future, anyone who wants to open a travel agency will first have to provide proof of his suitability for the job. (Note: time phrase at beginning or end; in future + future tense)
10. Ships used to be made of wood. (Note: Früher → used to)
11. With poached eggs, pierce the yolk beforehand/in advance.

12. Since the beginning of the semester, the number of students has fallen slightly.
13. They have been separated these last ten years.
14. The book hasn't arrived yet.
15. For the first time, a Russian will take part in a/the voyage of the manned spacecraft "Discovery".
16. The Minister has been suspended for the time being.
17. At nine (years of age), the otherwise good pupil was bottom of the class in German.

Consolidation

"The same procedure as every year, James", the senile Miss Sophie instructs her butler **(a) for the umpteenth time** in "Dinner for One". **(b) Year in, year out**, British restaurants **(c) have faithfully served up** food according to this principle. **(b) Up to now,** visitors from the Continent **(a) have been able** to profit from the maintenance of this tradition. Anyone who **(c) had ever learned** the words "kidney pie", "sausage", "cod", "chips", "cabbage", and "peas" wouldn't run into any kind of difficulty reading the local menu. But **(b) for some time now**, in London, time-honoured English cooking **(c) has increasingly been pushed aside** by so-called "Modern British Cuisine". Dishes with exotic names such as "Ben jang au" **(b) now bring** furrows even to the brows of professors of English. But what is hidden behind this new feasting trend?

Refreshing fruit salads, tender meat and crisp vegetables **(c) used to have** no place in English cuisine. "Fish 'n' chips" was the expression of British food culture. **(b) Since the late '60s**, however, **(a) there has developed** a rival to greasy halibut and chips with vinegar. Because a great number of fellow Commonwealth citizens **(b) moved** to the mother country and carried on their traditions and culinary arts there. African, far-eastern and eastern restaurants opened their doors everywhere in the capital.

Take your pick

a. Abbreviations

z.B. → e.g. → such as/for example
b.w. → p.t.o. → please turn over
d.h. → i.e. → that is
vgl. → cf. → compare

Betr. → Re → Referring to/Reference
i.A. → p.p. → on behalf of
usw. → etc. → and so on

b. geboren

1. b. I've known her since the day she was born. (Note: present perfect tense)
2. f. Where was she born? (Note: past tense)
3. a. She was born in Bielefeld. (Note: past tense)

4. g. Is he (an) American by birth? (Note: present tense)
5. i. He's a born liar.
6. c. He's a born artist.
7. d. He lives in Germany, but he's French by birth.
8. h. Her maiden name is Weil.
9. e. Christine Obersheimer, née Weil.

What else?

a. 1. eye 2. ear 3. cheek 4. nose 5. tooth
b. 1. face 2. shoulder 3. arm 4. chest 5. foot 6. leg 7. tail 8. back

Unit 5: Verbs referring to the present and the future

Lead-in

We are a producer of tents and tarpaulins for the German and French market. At the moment, we **are expanding** our range of large tents, as outdoor fairs and markets **are developing** rapidly. We **expect** a considerable increase in demand in the coming season.

We **are now seeking** dealers to introduce and sell our products in the UK. For this purpose, we **are going to appoint** a UK sales manager in January, so that dealers can be served directly from London. For every initial order of £2,000 or more, we **are offering** a 10% discount
(**Note**: the offer is open now. **Going to offer** would mean 'intend to offer (in the future)').

Should you be interested in the possibility of doing business with us in the future, we **will gladly arrange** for you to receive our detailed brochure.

I **look forward** to hearing from you.

(Signature)

P.S. As I **am representing** the company at the Camping and Leisure Fair in Leeds from 1st to 8th October, this would be an opportunity for us to meet directly at our stand in order to discuss any matters arising.

Follow-up

1. "Damn this siege! Just when "Star Trek" **is beginning** at home..."
2. The refuse disposal **comes** punctually at 9.30 every Tuesday.
3. The milk**'s boiling** over.
4. We don't expect (that) they**'ll be giving** us any more gifts.
5. Conservative MP Sir Richard Body **is considering** his resignation.
6. The gravitational force of the moon **amounts** to only about a fifth of that of the Earth.
7. He**'s studying** Spanish this semester.
8. Next time, though, I'm **going to** book first class!
9. Christmas Eve **falls** on a Saturday this year.
10. She always **allows** herself a sherry before lunch.

Consolidation

Paragraph 1 b; Paragraph 2 a; Paragraph 3 b.

Take your pick

a.
1. The discovery of BRCA 1 still doesn't represent a breakthrough **in** the area of cancer research.
2. The inflation rate fell **to** 2% in March.
3. Again, many new exhibitors were welcomed **at** the Autumn Trades Fair this year.
4. The cost of the restoration is estimated **at** around 3000 marks.
5. The number of victims has risen **to** 43.
6. I could give the lecture more fluently **in** German.

b.
by
zu Wasser und Lande: by land and sea
von Minute zu Minute: minute by minute

for
zu diesem Zweck: for this purpose
zum ersten Mal/letzten Mal: for the first/last time
zum Besten: for the best
(etwas) zum Frühstück essen: have (something) for breakfast

at
zu Hause: at home
zum Abschluss (der Konferenz): at the end (of the conference)
Tomaten zu 40pf das Stück: Tomatoes at 40 pfennigs each
zur Zeit: at the moment
zu diesem Zeitpunkt: at this point (in time)

in
zu Paaren: in couples/pairs
zu meiner Verteidigung: in my defence
zum Teil: in part

What else?

a. mind b. rights c. spoke – wheel d. wind e. tables
f. rough g. mountain – molehill h. wall i. life j. dislike

Unit 6: Verbs referring to the past

Lead-in

1. bought 2. had sat down 3. bought/had bought 4. had already been
5. was to be found 6. got 7. has cost

Follow-up

A.
1. Goethe **was born** in Frankfurt in 1749.
2. We **were just translating** a text about infrastructures when the computer **broke down**.
3. I **passed** my school-leaving exam in July 1980.
4. As a precaution, we **set off** as early as 5 o'clock in the morning.
5. When the insurance man **rang**, we **were lying** in the bath.
6. While we **were having** breakfast, Sesame Street **was** on TV.

B.
1. Let's not talk about chicken – **I've just got over** a salmonella poisoning!
2. We**'ve been living here** these last twenty years.

3. **I've been swotting away** for weeks in order to pass the exam.
4. May I drive for a while? **I've passed** my driving test!

C.
1. Of course, we wanted to visit you today – it's just that you**'d forgotten** to invite us.
2. The drivers **had been preparing** the delivery for several hours when we got the fax with the new orders.
3. By 1963, Kennedy **had polarised** (the) Americans in the battle over racial integration.
4. Before we set out on our holiday, we **had been studying** Spanish for several months.

Consolidation

a. Fear of landslides

Following the severe earthquake in Los Angeles, the fear of landslides **has been added** to the danger of further aftershocks. By Friday, the death toll **rose** (or: **had risen** (past perfect)) to 52.

According to a first detailed estimate, almost 6000 people **were injured** in last Monday's earthquake, 550 of them seriously. Around 4000 buildings **were destroyed** (Or: **have been destroyed** — 'resultative' present perfect: see next sentence) or severely damaged. 4700 inhabitants **have found** shelter in one of the reception areas. There **have been** over 1500 aftershocks, several of them with a strength of more than 5.0 on the Richter scale.

On Thursday, a hospital in Santa Monica **had to be evacuated**, due to severe damage. This means that six hospitals in the region **have been closed**.

b. Post-war Germany

The prerequisites for an economic recovery in West Germany **were considerably boosted** just by the establishment of the Bizone. Nevertheless, the western powers **did not carry out** the **long-planned** currency reform until after the decision **had been taken** (or: **was taken**) to set up a West German state. On 20th June 1948, the **now almost worthless** Reichsmark **was devalued** on a scale of 1:10; every West German **received** an initial sum of 40 Deutsche Mark per head, and later a further 20. At the same time, Erhard **gained** acceptance for a series of **economic** measures in the Economic Council. These **decisions** effectively bolstered the industrial upturn which **had already begun**. Already by the end of 1949, the prewar position **had been regained**. However, it was not until later that large sections of the population **benefited** from this development. True, the shop windows filled up again 'overnight', but prices **rose steeply** in the first months and unemployment figures **soared**.

Take your pick

a.

1. It will be hard to get a permit, to say nothing of financial support.
2. It says here: "Three times a day before mealtimes."
3. The directions tell you step by step how to implement the programme.
4. The form teacher told him he ought to give up his blackmailing activities right away.
5. The form teacher said, "Give up your blackmailing activities right away".
6. Obviously the President had been telling a lie (or: been lying) when he promised there would be no new taxes.

b.

1. According to NASA's plans, the debris from Skylab was certainly expected to fall into the sea, but the calculations proved to be wrong.
2. Admittedly, the plums were not yet completely ripe, but, for (the purpose of) baking a cake, they could be used immediately.
3. Admittedly, they buy fresh vegetables, but then they cook them for hours on end.
4. Get me a kilo of washing powder – without phosphate, that is.
5. She's very old – over 80, in fact.

What else?

1. Good-looking 2. seeks / is seeking 3. athletic 4. sense of humor
5. walks in the country 6. seeks 7. long-term relationship 8. slim

Unit 7: Modals and conditionals

Lead-in

1.c 2.a 3.b 4.c 5.b 6.b

Follow-up

1 We are determined to achieve the wage increase at any price.
2. She likes fish fingers and chips.
3. Unfortunately, she hasn't been able to reach him up to now.

4. The vents on the back must not be covered.
5. We don't have to go to school today.

6. bound   7. supposed   8. said   9. due   10. intended   11. meant

12. May I make a suggestion concerning the rules of procedure?
13. Could you take me as far as the town centre?
14. With a long period of absence, the housekey should best be handed over to neighbours or friends.
15. I would have too much money.
16. Antoine would never have become a great clown.
17. They feared that the Port of London would be cut up.
18. What other paths could advertising have taken?
19. Didn't Henry Moore stress that his works would have been impossible to imagine, but for the stone compositions of the megalithic era?
20. In Germany, profits from the resale of real estate are not taxed, if one waits / you wait at least two years before reselling.
21. If you have any further questions, your sleeping car attendant will be pleased to help you.
22. If I had had any idea how long our visitor would stay, I would have moved into a hotel.
23. If he had checked the machine regularly, it wouldn't have to be repaired now.
24. When (or: If) she considers the fate of her predecessors, she can't feel particularly delighted.
25. Had we bought a spare cartridge, we could have printed out the manuscript today.
26. Were we to have stayed one more day, we would have seen the Oscar presentations.
27. Had we stayed at home, we wouldn't have wet feet now.
28. Should the plutonium be weapons-grade material, new charges will have to be laid.
29. If parts are missing or damaged, please return the slip to us at the address given.
30. Choose one of the following topics.
31. They would build sandcastles all day long.

Consolidation

A.

1. If you want to see the time of day, press the button once.
2. If a fault occurs, it can often have been caused by a detail.
3. If the power fails or the mains plug is pulled out, the time of day is cancelled.
4. If a time longer than 60 minutes is input, the display appears in hours and minutes, e.g. 1 h 15.
5. If you repeatedly use a particular setting, you can store it with your microwave appliance and then conveniently call it up whenever you need it.

B.

Re: Your consignment No. 445/3

The above consignment has arrived 3 weeks late, due to the French rail strike. We now have a storage problem, as several other consignments also arrived this week. If 445/3 had arrived a day earlier, we would have transported it to Bremerhaven. If we still had the Bremen premises, we would have no difficulty. Unfortunately, this is not the case.

We will move the goods to our warehouse soon, if there is a large demand on our stock. If we had enough orders now, we'd shift some of our stock immediately.

In the meantime, we are allowed to store the goods at the docks, and we need not collect them before the end of the month. But we do need a dock storage permit, which has to be renewed daily at $150 per day. Could you tell us, please, whether you are prepared to pay this additional cost?

With best wishes,

Take your pick

Often, the context is needed to decide which of the senses of lassen is intended. But these English translations express highly probable meanings:

B.

1. Playing golf **allows** the President to forget all his worries about plans for the future.
2. I **made him** (or: **got him to**) do his homework every day.
3. If your appliance is faulty, you should contact your service technician and **have** the fault repaired.
4. She **let** (or: **allowed**) the water splash down on her skin.
5. We'll be happy if you **leave** everything as it is.
6. If you like, you can **leave** your spare key **with us**.
7. We **make** (or: **have**) them clean the building.
8. Just **leave** your old tyres **with us** – we'll dispose of them at no extra charge.
9. She **let** him go into the house.
10. This would **make** the manuscript up to 12 pages longer.
11. Apparently, the Germans don't **allow** even the recession to spoil (or: **let** even the recession spoil) their Christmas.
12. Don't **let** him twist you round his little finger!
13. Sooner or later you're going to **get** (yourself) inoculated.
14. Now he used all the means at his disposal to **get** separated from Anna.
15. **Let** the fruit tea draw for at least 6 minutes.

What else?

1.

a. Best translation.

b. Noun-noun compound ‘dyslexia diagnosis’ (= Legasthenie-Diagnose) is more German than English (See noun phrases); rund is untranslated.

c. ‘Diagnosed as’ (not ‘with’); plural noun (‘ages’) needed.

2.

a. Present tense (‘work’) wrong (‘Since the 1960s’ + present perfect; Unit 4)

b. Present tense (‘are working’) wrong (see (a)). Wrong use of conditional ‘would’ (Unit 7); ‘German’ comma after ‘methods’.

c. Best translation.

3.

a. Simple past (‘defined’) wrong (‘so far’ + present perfect needed; Unit 4); ‘should be’ (= sein sollen) suggests duty; obligation, ‘ought to be’ (better: ‘are said to be’).

b. Best translation.

c. Wrong preposition: ‘At (= In) the search for’; simple past (‘defined’) wrong (see a); ‘which cause’ fails to translate sollen (in verantwortlich sein sollen) (Unit 7); bislang is untranslated.

Unit 8: Negation

Lead-in

A. “You’re not Lenin at all ...!”

B. “And you’re only now telling me this? (Or: And you’re telling me this only now?) They looked so real ....”

C. At no time was there any danger to the population.

Follow-up

1. Do not add water to fillet of fish.
2. In St Lucia, the holidaymaker is still a welcome guest, not a necessary inconvenience.
3. His car is only one month old.
4. The manager didn’t appear until three o’clock in the afternoon.
5. There are no difficulties at all.
6. Is there any chance at all?
7. To prevent fire, do not expose this equipment either to rain or to moisture.
8. She couldn’t visit me either.
9. Under no circumstances may you drink this water.
10. On no account are the contents of the message stored.

Consolidation

Put an end to the censorship! No more lies!

The aliens have long since been dissected and cloned.

We all know that, in Roswell in 1947, neither a weather balloon nor a military aircraft fell from the sky. It was nothing other than a flying saucer with a crew of five on board! Four of the aliens were dead on the spot. Neither did the fifth crew member survive (or: The fifth crew member did not survive either) – thanks to the US Air Force.

Only now is an officer of the US Air Force speaking out:

"I had no choice. Never before had I to work under such pressure. We were threatened with reprisals – but now I'm not troubled by that any more. I'm 86 now and no longer afraid at all – of anything or anybody. Probably not for the rest of my life will I get rid of the deep guilt I feel about these creatures from space. Neither will I ever forget those deep, dark eyes. It's time for the truth."

"The aliens have long since been dissected and cloned."

Lecture in Ockstadt Community Hall, 14.6., 8.00p.m.

Take your pick

A.

a. of	b. of	c. on	d. on	e. in	f. in	g. at
h. on	i. on	j. on	k. to	l. in	m. to	

B.

a. at	b. for	c. after	d. for (Am.E.: on)		e. about	f. along
g. in	h. up	i. of	j. in	k. on	l. in	m. up

What else?

2.

a. **A**n **E**nglish legation, among whom is **H**ans **H**olbein the painter, arrives at the **C**ourt (or: court) of **C**leves.
b. **M**ore and more, politicians in **E**ast **A**sian countries are being criticised for their environmental policies.
c. **A**fter almost a hundred years, we know less than ever what a '**G**erman' film is.
d. **B**elfast is the only city on the **I**rish island on which the **I**ndustrial **R**evolution had a crucial influence.

3.
the **F**rankfurt **B**ook **F**air; the **S**outh **A**merican subcontinent; an island republic; **Q**uantum **T**heory; the **M**artian climate; a summer's day; the **C**hristian **D**emocratic **U**nion; the **R**oman **C**atholic **C**hurch; the **N**eolithic **R**evolution; the **F**rench language; a **C**hinese philosopher; the carbon dioxide problem

Unit 9: Relative clauses

Lead-in

The German Federal Parliament has decided that the right to vote of EU citizens is to be governed by the following rules:

EU citizens who live or are otherwise normally resident in the Federal Republic of Germany will, upon applying, have their names entered on the electoral roll.

This application must be submitted no later than 9 May, 19... to the local authority where the EU citizen is registered as a resident.

The EU citizen must specify the local authority in his/her country of origin on whose electoral roll his/her name was listed.

The EU citizen must undertake to exercise his/her right to vote only in the Federal Republic of Germany.

Follow-up

A.

1. 'Danzon' tells the story of Julia, whose great passion is dancing.
2. Here is a copy of the news magazine whose articles exposed the scandal.
3. The four youths who planted fire bombs in a department store last summer are appearing in court today.
4. It's the same association to whom we made a donation last year.
5. That's exactly the model (which) I've been looking for everywhere.
6. The sudden change in the weather has aggravated / is aggravating the situation for thousands of people who are camping in the open.
7. He is hosting guests by whom he has to be liked.
8. This is the cave in which the first wall paintings were discovered.
9. It's a matter of members of a sect for whom nothing apart from their guru is of importance.
10. A poster isn't successful only when the film (which) it advertises is of high artistic value.

B.

1. There aren't many motorways along the British coast, (a fact/situation) which makes travelling long and very arduous.
2. Above all, *Die Zeit* shapes opinions, which is the most important thing for a newspaper.
3. I don't know what 'forklift truck' is in Russian.
4. For his art gallery in Emden, Henri Nannen gives everything he can.
5. Everything he had ever put down in writing was now being used against him.
6. Everywhere in Nature, scientists are discovering what they understand by the word 'chaos'.

C.

1. Anyone who lives in a family faces a tough year (ahead).
2. We can give further help to anyone who knows just the name of his travel agent.
3. Make sure that no liquid can get inside the appliance.
4. We want our customers to be satisfied.
5. The probe launched into orbit in 1989 is no longer working.
6. Anyone arguing in this way confused cause and effect.
7. He's one of the few still writing in Yiddish today.
8. John is the last person to cause any trouble.

Consolidation

1. in which
2. in which
3. in which
4. whose
5. in which
6. who

Take your pick

1.

a. the stone-clad steel construction
b. the so-called world championship
c. the user-friendly computer programme

2.

a. Fortunately, I have my ...
b. When we were children, we had to ...
c. But after that, it was impossible ...
d. Actually, Fehmann hasn't been ...

3.

a. Each location should check whether it could be a destination for this group.
b. This man is not a terrorist but is only fighting for his rights.
Or: This man is not a terrorist: he is only fighting for his rights.
Or: This man is not a terrorist. He is only fighting for his rights.

4.
a. b. e. remain unpunctuated (= defining relative clauses).

Punctuate c. d. f. (= non-defining relative clauses):
c. The players, who are all very keen, will begin their season on Monday.
d. Herr Schubert, who has just returned from the Miami conference, is now writing his report.
f. Cafe Lange, which has coffee cream cake on Mondays, is just around the corner.

What else?

Directions for use

Insert your parking permit as indicated by the arrow.
Pay the amount shown. Your change will be returned.
Take out your change.
Retrieve your parking permit.
If you require a receipt, press this button.
You can halt the procedure at any time.
Should you find this machine out of order, press the call button.

Unit 10: Joiners

Lead-in

a. wie	b. sondern	c. Neben	d. Allerdings	e. Sobald	f. Zudem
1. as	2. but	3. Besides	4. though	5. As soon as	6. In addition

Follow-up

1. My flight simulator has the same altimeter as a Cessna.
2. The staging acquires a visual elegance such as one would hardly have thought possible.
3. This biological principle applies as it did thousands of years ago.
4. The next Market Day is not – as we wrongly reported in yesterday's issue – on the 27th January, but on Friday, 7th January.
5. Afterwards, she couldn't explain herself how she had managed it.
6. She doesn't want to be disturbed while the lottery numbers are being drawn.
7. What does the cameraman feel while he's filming?
8. Do not store anything in the oven while the appliance is being used (or: while using the appliance).

9. In Northern Europe, real amber can be acquired without any difficulty, whereas this turns out to be problematic in North African countries.
10. Since (Or: As) he didn't have a road map on him, he frequently had to ask the way.
11. We cannot take any new orders at the moment as (or: since) our office is under severe pressure of work.
12. Our office in Australia is in constant touch with our German branch in Munich, so that an exchange of information is guaranteed at all times.
13. Your attendant will be pleased to take care of all customs formalities so that you are not (or: will not be) disturbed during the night.
14. We were never ill, although our life-style was very unhealthy.
15. At least, leave us our identity papers!
16. In spite of days and days of discussion, the workgroups weren't able to offer anything concrete.
17. The French don't want to intensify co-operation within the EU, but would far rather leave it as it is.
18. The sky darkened as if the end of the world were imminent.
19. He felt as if a hot bullet (had) penetrated his stomach.
20. On Saturday evening we'll go either to the cinema or to the theatre.
21. We need charcoal as well as mustard.
22. The children take on all jobs possible in order to scrape together the necessary money.
23. a. We're going ski-ing again in winter too/as well.
    b. We're also going ski-ing in winter again.
24. a. I'd like a salad too/as well.
    b. I'd also like a salad.

Consolidation

by Recorded delivery

As we have already informed you by phone, the above consignment was unloaded not in Valparaiso, as directed, but in Punta Arenas.
Since (Or: As) all the required shipment documents, including the bill of lading, show Valparaiso as the receiving port, the delivery error can only have resulted from a mistake by EXPRESS LINES, whom you represent.
Therefore, we hereby hold you fully responsible both for the costs resulting from this delivery error and for all further possible losses which may occur. At the moment, our client cannot specify the exact amount of the resulting costs. As soon as the appropriate figures are known, we shall pass these on to you.
Moreover, we would be interested to know the reason for the misdirected delivery of the 4 cases. In the meantime, therefore, please advise us of the result of the investigations of the shipowner in the importing country.

With best wishes, (Hans Dechert)

Take your pick

Kitsch: yes	Angst: yes	Lederhosen: yes
Bürgermeister: no (mayor)	Schnaps: yes	Autobahn: no (Am.E.: highway. Br.E.: motorway)
Rucksack: yes	Zeitgeist: yes	Wurst: Am.E.: yes. Br. E.: no (sausage)
Wanderlust: yes	Rathaus: no (Am.E.: city hall. Br.E.: town hall)	
Poltergeist: yes	Sauerkraut: yes	

Note:

a. Often, a German word is used in English when it refers only to Germany or to Germans. Example: 'Take the autobahn to Kassel then head to towards Fulda'.

b. When you use a borrowed word in English, do not underline or capitalise it. Example: kindergarten, not Kindergarten.

What else?

Who's calling?
Name & location?
Specify exactly the location of the accident.
What has happened?
Number of sick or injured?
Are the injured trapped?

Emergency call

Unit 11: Passives & *Es*-sentences

Lead-in

There are two kinds of Postbank savings schemes: Type A and Type B. The difference lies in the way the interest is paid out.

With **Type A**, for the whole investment period – which may be 4 or 6 years, according to your choice – you are guaranteed the rate of interest which was current when the contract was signed. A minimum deposit of 5000 DM is required. The annual interest is added to the capital and they earn further interest together. So, at the end of the investment period, you receive the nominal value together with the interest and the compound interest.

With **Type B**, likewise, for the whole investment period – which may be 4 or 6 years – you are guaranteed the rate of interest which was current when the contract was signed. Here, too, a minimum deposit of 5000 DM is required. With Type B, though, interest is paid both at the end of each calendar year and at the end of the investment period.

Follow-up

1. Passives:

1. The health risks are still being discussed.
2. Even Eurocheques are accepted here.
3. Obviously, the educational function the libraries have (or: of the libraries) isn't being recognised at all.
4. A notice is being sent to you about this.
5. Now the King is seizing the initiative himself and is being supported in this by his Parliament.
6. Baby food in jars or bottles is always to be heated without a lid.
7. Modern Turkey cannot be understood without the reforming achievements of Ataturk.
8. He should be ashamed of himself!
9. Host families for young people from Italy are being sought by the Association as well.
10. No further residue could be traced.
11. What can you do about it?
12. The door to the office is half-open, and you can hear the staff talking in the corridor.

2. Es-sentences

1. There's no finer place on Earth.
2. There are English-speaking staff in some travel agents and hotels.
3. It's a question of money.
4. It's also possible to use a flat dish.
5. Between 1960 and 1991, there were 12 tax increases.
6. This time he succeeded at the first attempt.
7. I was sorry that we'd caused her any difficulty.
8. The time for getting the dissertation finished is slowly drawing near.
9. Nothing remained but to pack his things and take off.
10. Everything succeeds with him.
11. The question is whether an intervention would really be sensible.
12. Britons are much more suspicious when it comes to assessing the EU's influence on everyday life in the member states.

3. A question of style:

Correct order: I. E*. H*. B*. A. F*. G. D. C*.
Of the 9 parts, 5 (marked *) use the pronoun **you/your.**

Consolidation

Day ticket
Correct order: (f) (j) (h) (g) (c) (e) (l) (b) (k) (a) (d) (i)

The English translation, written in full, is as follows:

Day ticket
You may use a day ticket from the time you cancel it up to 6.00a.m. the following day.
The **single day ticket** is valid for one person.
The **partner day ticket** is valid for five persons (of whom up to two may be over 18 years old) and one dog. An unlimited number of your own children up to 17 years old may accompany you free of charge, if you can show that they are yours.
Single and partner day tickets for the **City Area** are also available as **3-day tickets**.

Take your pick

1. They should look after each other better.
2. Avoid placing several layers of different foods on top of each other.
3. The two of them stuck to each other although they had never been able to stand one another.
4. They walked alongside each other, at pains to remain level.
5. The pupils can't distinguish letters like b and d from each other.
6. The project required everyone to work with each other.

What else?

A.

Nanook of the North

1922 documentary film about the life of Nanook the Eskimo and his family in the Arctic.

The documentary filmmaker Robert Flaherty spent several months in the deepest Arctic and let his camera run, while the Eskimo Nanook and his family went about the business of their everyday life. From fishing to building the igloo together, Flaherty documented the entire daily routine of a people who even now are little known to us. The film which emerged from this is still today considered to be the most outstanding documentary of the silent film era.

B.

Citizen Kane

An American Dream comes true.

"Rosebud". The media mogul C.F. Kane (Orson Welles) utters the strange word and dies. What did he mean? Reporter Jerry Thompson (William Alland) wants to find out and questions friends of the millionaire. Through their accounts, Kane's eventful life and the contradictory facets of his character are unwound by means of flashbacks.

Because Hearst the publisher, in 1940, saw clear parallels to his own life, he tried to take possession of the film material – without success. ZDF is showing this most outstanding of films and Orson Welles' debut production, on the occasion of his 80th birthday on 6th April.

Unit 12: Expressions of quantity

Lead-in

The English versions of the headlines appear at various points in the unit:
Reduced goods – you save up to 30%.
At any price
Your answer is worth all of 5,000DM to us.
(The) interest rate has fallen to 7.2%!
Two thirds (of the population) commute to work.
Architects' fees rise by five percent.
Lando (is) the most successful racehorse of all time.
(The) number of receivers (has) doubled.
Victory in the 90th minute.
Kohl turns 65 – Congratulations from all around the world.

Follow-up

A.

1. If you want to stop a process ahead of time, press the cancellation button twice.
2. Since 1985, the number of complaints about noise pollution has doubled.
3. Women represented about three-quarters of the unemployed.
4. In the last two decades, the number of road deaths in Germany has fallen by 58 percent.
5. We're reckoning with an increase of ten to twelve percent on last year's turnover of 52 million marks.
6. 80% of the tickets for the January performances and more than 60% of those for February have already been sold.
7. I've put on half a kilo since the weekend!

B.

1. The Garrick in Covent Garden is (or: ranks) among the most superior clubs in the British capital.
2. Since 1960, petrol tax has grown from the seventh- to the third-highest tax, according to the Institute.

3. The property has (or: comprises) an area of four hectares.
4. We need DM3600 a month on average (or: an average of DM3600 a month).
5. A large pile of rubbish adorned his front garden.
6. We turned five kilos of potatoes into chips.
7. Would you bring us three bottles of beer, please?
8. In Germany, you come of age on your 18th birthday.

C.

1. In the referendum, the whole population declared itself opposed to his idea.
2. Try to comprehend this culture as a whole.
3. He gave her not quite a hundred marks.
4. It can be better to warm up two portions one after the other than both at the same time.
5. Neither of them worked for the KGB.
6. Both of them had removed cutlery from East German canteens.
7. Not all automobiles have a fifth gear.
8. This disinfectant kills all known bacteria.
9. All the EU member states signed the treaty.
10. All the reserve players were hoping for their big chance.
11. The hamburgers were anything but edible.

D.

1. Each individual Mah-jong piece was hand-carved.
2. Two in every three Europeans have no interest in sport.
3 Of course, any boss would like to have a Minibar like this.
4. Australia is further away from Europe than any other place in our global village.
5. Some people dream all their life of being independent.
6. We bought this house some 30 years ago.

Consolidation

A.

- The oil crisis of 1973 made many Europeans use energy more economically in the home.
- 47% reduced their heating costs by means of improved insulation, 39% simply use less heating, and 44% switch on lights and domestic appliances less frequently.
- Taken altogether, energy consumption in the EU has fallen by 13% in the last 15 years.
- Seen as a whole, though, there has been an increase in the consumption of electricity.

B.

Energy consumption in private households.
Energy use in an average private household in percent (1994)

An average private household consumes around 45,000 kilowatt hours (kw/h) of energy in a year. Over half of this is used up by heating. So keeping rooms warm accounts for 53 percent of energy consumption. The car uses up a third, and so is the second-biggest devourer of energy. On the other hand, only seven percent is accounted for by electrical appliances – from the light bulb to the drier – on the overall energy balance sheet. The same amount is accounted for by hot water.

Take your pick

1. little 2. a little 3. few 4. a few 5. few 6. little
7. have fewest cars in proportion to
8. is little probability that the
9. is hardly less of a problem than
10. was embellished with a bit of luxury

What else?

economics: 4. (English singular nouns ending in -s)
earphones, binoculars: both 2. (German singular nouns → English plural nouns)
government, class: both 3. (English nouns which can be singular or plural)
knowledge: 1. (German count nouns → English mass nouns)

Unit 13: Controlling the sentence

Lead-in

1a. 2b. 3a. (For the rationale for these choices, see **'How to' guidelines.**)

Follow up

1. It takes more than a day to travel to Australia.
2. It is important first to analyse the financial means available.
3. What is fascinating is the great variety of fauna in this country.
4. What might receive recognition is a minimum of five years employment in a travel agency.

5. What's important is what he and others are doing to solve our problems.
6. We need a forceful plan of action to get human rights accepted.
7. What did not conform to Indian caste attitudes was not accepted by British colonial society either.
8. Certainly, economic interests are still the highest priority in the relationship between Europe and Japan.
9. There can be no doubt that Japanese investments in Europe have brought Asia and the Old World closer together.
10. Japanese companies have gained an excellent reputation by the way they treat their European employees and the way they co-operate with the various local communities.
11. With a convincing air of innocence, the two teenagers smuggled weapons-grade plutonium to Rosbach every day.

Consolidation

Text A: One day after autumn had begun, the Pastor of Perlin had his bay saddled, mounted it and rode in a leisurely fashion over to the Pogreß estate. He had asked Frau Römer, the tenant farmer's wife, to let him have a word in private with Johanne, their second daughter. The girl had turned seventeen in June. She seemed to the Pastor to be graceful and prudent, as well as capable about the house. Until this morning he had been sure that she was favourably disposed towards him. He was beginning to have doubts now, although not many. It would turn out as God wished. Everything turned out that way. Mankind lived by this law and by the rules of the authorities ordained by God. Anyone who knew this had taken the first step towards worldly wisdom. Worldly wisdom was the path to worldly bliss.

Text B: One March morning, Eckenpenn got up very early. During the night, his landlord – or the husband of his landlady – had come home late, furious in his drunkenness. As usual in cases like this, it had turned into a battle between the three of them – Frau Lehnert, her daughter Hermine and Lehnert, the drunk carpenter. This time Hermine took her mother's side. Last time, about ten days earlier, she had stood by her father. She divided her strength equally between her parents and thereby maintained on both sides a loving understanding for the periods of sobriety, during which Frau Lehnert was in charge of everything. She did the washing. Lehnert occasionally drank varnishing spirit.
For some time, the second-hand book dealer had lain awake and eavesdropped with dreary reluctance. Nor later did sleep return to him with its continuous, dark cover, but it was as if, by turns, black and light wings were beating down, and a multitude of gluttonous dreams flapped about his brow. Besides this, he really felt the cold. March had brought an icy chill around the beginning of spring.

Take your pick

A.

1. children's rights
2. a friend of mine
3. Henry's six wives
4. a year's leave
5. the inventor of the first flying machine
6. a week's holiday
7. at the butcher's
8. the Jones' daughters
9. the cause of his illness
10. several of Robin's books
11. the events of the Second World War
12. the leopard's spots
13. the leader of the newly-formed Social Democrats

B.

1. Unfortunately, his dream of having a swimming pool of his own (or: his own swimming pool) could not be realised.
2. Without a car of my own, I can't take on this job.
3. Since he has had a computer of his own (or: his own computer) at his disposal, he has hardly been seen at all in the university.

What else?

1. Later that afternoon, however many times she rang his office, he was still unavailable.
2. He didn't believe in changes and was indeed, as long as he wasn't threatened, against changes.
3. What might he have said anyway?
4. Mrs Andrew is not particularly excited and certainly not amused by all this.
5. Thin, very thin limbs beneath the excellent suit, and very hairy; in the very first minutes of his life he had already needed this protection (or: already in the ...).
6. She took the man back to her room; it wasn't in fact hers any longer.
7. She felt a cold coming on as something to be welcomed and yet resented.
8. What am I supposed to do with a sewing machine? You couldn't sew fur jackets with it in any case.
9. It would be even better if the records played a little longer, but the contraption isn't all that big.
10. They had left no letter, doubtless because they couldn't agree on one version.
11. They call it the Hunter's Moon, because September is the huntsman's season, I suppose.
12. He knows very well that his party cannot prop up such a programme alone.